Divorce Matters

Get the divorce that works for you.

A practical guide for you to discover what you really want and plan for your best future.

This book is not exhaustive. It has been designed to stimulate the thought process and provide a base for what you could consider.

ELIZABETH GODDARD

Divorce Matters

Get the divorce that works for you.

A practical guide for you to discover
what you really want and plan for
your best future.

ELIZABETH GODDARD

DIVORCE MATTERS | Get the divorce that works for you.
A practical guide for you to discover what you really want and plan for your best future.

This edition is published by
Revive Your Soul Publishing in 2023 © Copyright 2023
Elizabeth Goddard All rights reserved.

ISBN: 978-1-9163577-4-7

I dedicate this book to:
The wounds that need healing
To the children
To the life ahead of you.

Acknowledgement: Whilst researching for a YouTube video, I came across a worksheet which transformed this book from 'Three Things you Should Never do when Divorcing a Narcissist' to 'Divorce Matters'.

During the video, I went through the worksheet and spoke about my experiences and how different it would be with an emotional abuser. I offered other ideas to help with negotiation and support.

www.divorcepeacenegotiators.com/wp-content/uploads/2013/06/Divorce-Settlement-Checklist.pdf

Divorce Matters

WELCOME

My name is Elizabeth, and I am so glad you have decided to join me on this part of your journey. I want to help you inner-stand (the inner knowing; it is your intuition, the unarguable knowledge that something is true) why it hurts so much and hold a safe space for you.

For the majority of women and men, it is not until the relationship is over that they start to question if it was healthy. Emotional Abuse is horrific and affects every area of your life. When the relationship ends it might be the hardest thing you have had to deal with. Just as you start to reclaim some energy, take tentative steps to rebuild your life, and realise your brain is starting to function a little better, you are faced with divorce.

Why are these types of relationships so hard to heal from?

The damage caused puts you into such a state of confusion that you had no idea the abuse was taking place; like Chinese water torture, it happened very, very slowly and it turned you insane.

Your ex has already negotiated in their head what you are now worth to them, and, if you are not ready for their games, they can take advantage of you and manipulate the process, using it to gain attention and hurt you.

So, hold on tight for the ride of your life.

Elizabeth x

"

Nice people don't
necessarily fall in love with
nice people

- Jonathan Franzen

"

CONTENTS

DIVORCE MATTERS

Divorce isn't a pleasant experience, full stop. It is the ending of something, and unless you both came to that decision, there will be one person who has to come to terms with a decision their partner has made. They have to catch up emotionally with this decision. When something ends and one person isn't expecting it, they may feel out of their comfort zone, trying to make sense of what is happening.

But when that person has been in an abusive relationship, it isn't about getting to the same point that your partner is. That doesn't exist, because you may have started to discover that the relationship you thought you were in didn't exist and the person you thought they were doesn't, either.

An emotionally healthy partner will offer information, trying to help their partner, in whatever way they can, to accept that the relationship is no longer working. Closure is rare in an emotionally abusive relationship, as it serves no purpose to the abuser. It means you get to walk away, and by not giving you closure, it allows them to maintain control and power.

During the process, you might see glimpses of the person you remember, the person you fell in love with, the person you thought was protecting you. The one that told you how perfect you were together. The one who told you that you were soul mates. The one who told you that you were the only person who had ever understood them – and then walked away, leaving you broken.

Divorce Matters!
Emotionally healthy people do not want to hurt you; emotionally unhealthy ones do.

Divorce Matters.
It will be an important part of the process; you can get the closure you need and heal the emotional wounds.

Your **Divorce Matters** are important as well: get all the information you need, dot all the i's and cross all the t's and start to create the life you deserve to live.

The abuse can start all over again with the divorce, and the Abuser will recycle the knowledge they have learned about you for their pleasure.

The divorce process is the perfect playground for the Emotional Abuser to have some fun. It is in full view of everyone, and they get great pleasure from causing you pain whilst they lament in front of their audience.

When you see a word in CAPITAL LETTERS you will find a reference to it in the chapter The A-Z of Emotional abuse.

START HERE

This book has many purposes and is not exhaustive.

The aim is to give you a framework and encourage you to think about areas you might not have initially considered.

You might hear phrases like 'we don't need legal help', 'we can sort this out ourselves', or 'they are just after your money'. These should be RED FLAGS to you.

I also hope this process will give you permission to ask the questions you need to ask, the questions you may be scared to ask and the questions you have been told you don't need to ask.

Take a deep breath, turn each page, read each question, and then write. No one but you has to see this. Be honest and raw and don't worry about your grammar or spelling.

If your answer is NO to a question, use it to go inwards and state what you would like or how you would see this area finalising. For example, if you haven't discussed or finalised child custody (if relevant), use the box to write out what you want and what is in the best interest of the child or children.

If you have discussed an area, remember it isn't finalised until the agreement is signed, so listen to your body and hear what it has to say.

At the back of the book, I have included a chapter you can use to collect the information you need and areas you need to negotiate. You might need to adjust certain sections for your own specific needs. There are blank pages at the end of each section for your notes or questions.

Make sure you have all your paperwork in order and prepare for the games to commence.

This workbook has been designed to support your legal assistance, not to replace any legal advice.

EMOTIONAL ABUSE

You will not get closure, so it is helpful to 'INNER-STAND' what and why you feel the way you do and understand what comes next and the healing that needs to be done.

Emotional Abuse is insidious.

Unlike physical ABUSE, it often goes unnoticed, and the damage it causes puts you into a state of confusion. You had no idea it was taking place, and like Chinese water torture, it happened very slowly and turned you crazy.

EMOTIONAL ABUSE is a pattern of behaviour: one person uses fear, humiliation, guilt or manipulation tactics to gain power over another.

It affects every area of your life: physically, mentally, emotionally, spiritually and financially and it is hard not only to walk away but to recover from. They chipped away at your self-esteem, and you began to doubt your perceptions and reality.

The ABUSER used many tactics to trap you and to gain power and control over you, your life and your finances.

They manipulated you into believing they were protecting you.

The CYCLE OF ABUSE is made up of three elements: idealisation, devaluation and discard. Each element is carried out with precision for the abuser's desired results.

You are left with your life in chaos and the ABUSER walks away without a backward glance, having secured in place their next source of SUPPLY (this is attention, and the abusers surround themselves with people who can provide it to them - a more detailed explanation is at the end of the book).

You may be at this point trying to understand what happened; you may be trying to label the ABUSER.

You very possibly experienced idealisation, where you were the centre of their world. They told you how amazing you were and showered you with gifts and meals and days out.

Over a period of time, this changed. Suddenly the things they loved about you were turned against you. The words of idealisation became criticism and put-downs.

This was followed by the discard. It was temporary at first; they always came back with the attention you were used to. You sighed with relief, and you may have vowed to yourself you wouldn't let that happen again.

They have one goal, and that is power and control. You will be in their life UNTIL you are no longer fit for purpose – that could be a short period of time or a long one. When they have enough enticement and a new shiny toy appears, off they go.

The aim of the game was to bond you to them, so you couldn't reject them or abandon them. TRAUMA BOND is designed to trap you; it has invisible chains holding you in the relationship, unable to move or escape.

You were lured with fakery and then held there in an invisible prison. They have the key but they will never give it to you – not even at the end of the relationship. Whilst there is still a breath in your body, you have the ability of providing them with a source or SUPPLY.

EMOTIONAL DIVORCE

Being emotionally divorced will change the way you negotiate, and one of the best things you can do is reframe the way you view this divorce: remove all emotion and start to see this process as a contract.

I believe that knowledge is power, and by understanding the games they play and 'inner-standing' the wounds and bonds that might trap you, you can change the way you respond.

And responding is key in this: from the very first moment you met they were listening to you, making mental notes on what is important to you, and this information will be used to get you to react. This is another thing you can change when you divorce emotionally.

You might be experiencing rumination, and are caught and trapped with your thoughts, wondering 'WHAT IF and MAYBE'. What if you had said something differently? If you hadn't said or done something, would you still be here, believing this was all your fault?

Healing the trauma bond is crucial

If you still have the trauma bond intact, this could be detrimental to you and your future.

We develop bonds for survival in childhood, usually with our caregiver, who is the foundation of attachment. When our safety is threatened in some way, we turn to them for support and protection.

TRAUMA BONDING is one of the reasons it is so hard to heal from toxic and emotionally abusive relationships. Bonding happens in all relationships, but this type of bonding was one-sided, and this is why it was so easy for them to walk away, as they didn't BOND to you.

Bonding is a very strong connection, and it strengthens when we spend time with someone, when we make love, and when we have children together. TRAUMA bonding is used by the Emotional Abuser to gain power and control over you

TRAUMA BONDING made it hard to enforce BOUNDARIES, which is why it is so painful to stay away from them. When they threatened your safety through their bad behaviour, you turned to them for help and protection, rationalising their behaviour, believing they cared about you, creating further bonding – which is the reason you feel so connected to them.

When the relationship finished, your stress levels were so high, you couldn't imagine your life without them.

Grieving the past, the present and the future.

Grieving is such an important step in your healing, and you might not even realise you need to grieve.

Grief isn't just about the loss of a person; it can be a relationship or a job.

In these relationships, it is more complex. You were presented with a persona that wasn't real. The way you felt was very real, however: you might have been seen or heard for the very first time or in a way no one has ever treated you in your life.

During the idealisation stage, they listened very carefully to what you were looking for in a relationship and in a partner. They created and presented this to you during the relationship, and this is why you don't recognise them when the relationship breaks down. You need to grieve the persona – the person you thought they were.

You will also need to grieve the present; you never thought you would be here. This wasn't part of the plan. You invested so much of yourself, your time and your money. Perhaps you gave up everything for them; you may have changed for them. Grieve for those moments when you wanted to walk away, to leave, to end the relationship and you decided to stay when you saw a glimmer of hope – when you heard the excuse for their bad behaviour and chose to forgive them once more.

As well as the present, you will need to grieve the future: the fake one you created together. This is another reason you stayed longer than you intended.

It takes time to untangle yourself from the invisible chains that held you there.

You know more than you think you know!

If anything, they are more than a little predictable and you really do know more than you think you do.

During the relationship, they told you that you were the only person who ever understood them. You saw how they treated other people but thought they would never do that to you.

There is only one outcome that matters, and that is to win at any cost – even by a penny. And if they know something is important to you, they will either want it or they will want to destroy it.

When you sit down and work through areas such as your assets, consider what each item is worth to them. This process will help you negotiate.

If your children are a high priority for you, the abuser will make sure they are for them. If you are dividing assets, contemplate which ones will be important or be worth more. Would you rather have your children an extra day as a swap for the better car?

Don't get caught up arguing over something you will later be staring at that reminds you of the divorce process, what it cost you in time and money – and what it cost you mentally and emotionally.

When you list your assets, put a letter against it of how important it is to you and what you would be willing to hand over. In **COLUMN A**, put the things that are non-negotiable for you. Use **COLUMN B** for the things you might be willing to give up or negotiate on. **COLUMN C** is for everything that you are happy for them to win.

This list is for your eyes only.

When splitting money and assets, if they are in a better financial position, ask for more than you would be happy to settle with. They will negotiate down, never up.

They don't care about you, they just care about what they get out of the process.

Image is important. They don't like people to think badly of them and they will need to leave the process winning, even if it is by just a small amount.

Be careful not to get caught in their games

It might not be the same quality but if they get bored, they can play with you like a cat plays with a dead mouse. If you have ever seen a cat with a mouse, you may have noticed they tap it to get a response, or they throw it in the air and then chase it. In the abuser's world, this is called HOOVERING.

They are 'just checking you are OK'. They have realised they can't live without you. They are hurting. They need you. They don't want you going through this alone. And the list goes on.

The abuser will tell you they don't want you using your money on legal fees, but this is not for the reason they claim. They may start saying this very early on, like an earworm working its way into your thoughts. You might believe the abuser is doing this to protect you, but really it is because you having a representation isn't part of their plan. If you were to instruct a legal team, the abuser starts to lose control.

A legal team wasn't part of the negotiation that took place in their head. They are going to ask too many questions, and as they will be working for you they **should** have your interests in their focus – which means they are not the best for the Emotional Abuser.

If you do instruct a team, the abuser may try and undermine your relationship with them, questioning their motives, possibly asking you 'who is advising you of this', getting you to question everything. Gaslighting you again. Leaving you wondering, 'Were they right, should you be listening to your representation?' 'Perhaps you have got this all wrong.'

You might ask yourself if there is something wrong with you and if they were right all along.

They do not want anyone else to control the divorce other than themselves; they do not even want their legal team to be in charge.

You might also hear statements like 'I don't want to fight'. What they actually mean is they don't want **you** to fight; they want you to agree with them and accept their demands. They want to control everything. Or they might say 'I want this to be amicable'. Or perhaps you might hear 'I don't want you wasting your money on legal fees'.

You might hear statements like 'We don't need legal help'. The Emotional Abuser doesn't want you to get legal help and you need to be really careful, particularly if you still believe they care for you or wouldn't do anything to hurt you.

The abuser wants it to look amicable, for them to look good, so they can win everyone round to their way of thinking, and they will use language and words to trigger you.

They would love nothing better if you start to lose control of your emotions, and they can claim you are the crazy one they have told everyone about.

The divorce process is a stage, a place for them to gain the supply they need.

They like to cause drama and play the victim.

They don't care about you, they just care about what they get out of the process.

It is important for you to 'INNER-STAND' who is running the divorce.

During the idealisation period, they learnt about you, your likes and dislikes and what is important to you. They use this information to get a reaction from you, and for them, it is a simple equation: reaction equals supply.

They will deliberately try to get a reaction from you, and by 'inner-standing' where you have been hurt and healing the wounds, you can respond rather than react.

This also helps you start to claim back your power and get the divorce that works for you.

Trust your intuition.

Set BOUNDARIES and make sure you stick to them. Check in with yourself and ask how you feel and if this is really what you want. The real cost of divorce is to your mental and emotional, physical and spiritual health and that of your children if you have them, as well as the financial impact of the divorce itself.

HOW TO DIVORCE EMOTIONALLY

You will not get closure, so it is helpful to 'INNER-STAND' what and why you feel the way you do, and understand what comes next and the healing that needs to be done.

You might be put off by the word 'healing' and see it as woo woo or of a spiritual nature, like OM-ing at the top of a mountain.

With emotional abuse comes emotional scars. The wounds that are created are much like physical wounds, except they're invisible. This pain is very real.

You are in control of how you do this, and you can even choose to not do it.

I have included a section at the back to help with your recovery and help you Divorce Emotionally.

Remember

You may still be trapped. This might be due to the CYCLE OF ABUSE when they discarded you on a regular basis as part of the TRAUMA BONDING.

Each time they came back (they leave emotionally rather than physically), they idealised you: they were so sorry, they realised how important you are and how much the relationship means to them. Only this time, they haven't come back. But you were trained to wait, and you might be stuck here waiting.

Make it your priority to Divorce Emotionally from the abuser before you go into the negotiation with them.

This is a power game, and the TRAUMA BOND will keep you trapped and submissive during this process.

A warrior doesn't go to battle unfit for the challenge, a boxer doesn't get into the ring unprepared for their fight and a runner doesn't start a race without making sure they have run a few miles. You shouldn't do it, either.

Prepare yourself emotionally, mentally, physically and spiritually.

Healing the wounds and the pain means you are in a better place to question their motives, you are in a better place to negotiate and you are in a better place to make decisions that are best for you.

Who or what is running your divorce?

Emotional abuse penetrates so many levels, so many layers; your brain was tricked to believe what you were told was the truth. It takes time to detraumatise, and it is so easy to slip back down the dark hole when faced with new facts or new situations. You were never going to get the closure you needed – and that is part of the game.

GASLIGHTING is really dangerous, creating feelings of Insecurity, Confusion, Brain Fog, Self-doubt, Fear, Not Feeling Good Enough and Feeling Vulnerable or Powerless.

Your legal team doesn't live with you, and they are not watching what is happening in your life. You need to highlight any manipulative behaviour to them.

An emotionally abusive person behaves in a selfish way. They are higher up on the narcissistic spectrum. Some are easier to spot than others: they have a grandiose sense of importance and an insatiable need for admiration, wealth, power or fame. They lack empathy and consideration for others.

Above all, they are children in an adult's body, unable to take responsibility for any of their actions, and anyone who disagrees with them or their unreasonable expectations might be subjected to their narcissistic rage.

Because their needs were unmet during childhood, they were unable to master critical emotional development. I discovered many years ago that you could understand the age in which their trauma happened: in certain situations they reverted to child-like behaviour. If you think back, you may recall that when they were threatened or they perceived danger, they may have walked or talked in a childish way.

I know you are hurting and have been for a long time, but NOW is the time to fall back in LOVE with you! The only person you are responsible for is yourself.

You may believe you can help them, after all. You may still believe you are the only one who has ever understood them fully, but you sadly can't.

They may have agreed to relationship counselling, but unless the counsellor has experience working with personality-disordered people, they may believe the abuser's stories, and you'll leave wondering what happened and believing this is all your fault.

You have been left broke and broken, picking up the pieces. The fairy tale is over, and you now have to fight your way out of the dark forest and back to safety.

You might have left yourself a trail of breadcrumbs and have been able to follow that out. The nightmare is coming to an end, and you no longer wake up fighting them off you or crying yourself to sleep or waking up crying. You are starting to laugh a little. But just as you are starting to rebuild your life, the sequel arrives... Ding ding! Round 2. The Divorce!

Virtually nobody is untouched by divorce, from your children through to friends and family.

There is always a cost, and it is not only financial.
There is a cost to the children.
There is a cost of emotional pain.
You might have lost everything.
You might find you are left with debts.
You might be discovering the person you believed you were married to didn't actually exist.

Emotionally healthy people make mistakes, and their marriages do break down. They do have affairs and they may possibly try and work through this and then realise the hurt party can't move on, so they separate and divorce, they grow apart and decide that marriage isn't for them.

Emotionally healthy people want to ensure the other party gets closure and they do everything in their power to split everything equally, knowing how important it is for both of them.

Emotionally unhealthy people don't!

Manipulation is a tool they use regularly, and you will have experienced this in your relationship.

Abusers are masters of manipulation. They use words to deceive, coerce, seduce and mislead you to gain power and control.

It doesn't matter who wants the divorce; the emotional abuser will assess what value it holds and then will use the process. They will use it to gain power and control over you and they know how much supply they will get from this process.

If you want to fight for what is legally yours, they will respond through manipulation.

If you make an offer, this will be seen as you trying to take control.

In the relationship, what was yours was theirs and what was theirs was theirs – and this carries over into the divorce process. They cannot take responsibility, therefore this is all your fault. If they had an affair, it was because of you, and they use their bad behaviour and flip it to something you did.

There is a whole new level of mindfuckery that goes on. If you want the divorce, they will delay it, sitting on paperwork and not agreeing with anything.

They will hide assets and fabricate allegations. Anything they did to you becomes what you did to them. They will dispute experts and they don't want you to get any legal help. They smear your character and you may read things about yourself that are completely untrue.

They need to be in control.

They will not give you what you want.

There are only two things guiding this: the amount of supply they can gain and the amount of power and control they have over the process. They don't care what happens to you, or to your finances during this process, or the effect it has on the children and the fact that the money you are using to pay for representation could go towards the children having a better quality of life.

They pull on their victim mask and manipulate.

The divorce process is not hard.
It is MADE hard.

They need to win at any cost, and this will be financial but it could also be mental and emotional.

They don't care about you, they just care about what they get out of the process.

It is important for you to 'INNER-STAND' who is running the divorce: during the idealisation period, they learnt about you, your likes and dislikes and what is important to you.

And they use this information to get a reaction from you. For them it is a simple equation: reaction equals supply.

They will deliberately try to get a reaction from you and by 'inner-standing' where you have been hurt and the wounds you have, you can respond. This also helps you start to claim back your power and get the divorce that works for you.

Trust your intuition.

Find a tribe that knows how to support you through this.

Set BOUNDARIES and make sure you stick to them. Check in with yourself and ask how you feel and if this is really what you want. The real cost of divorce is to your mental, emotional, physical and spiritual health – and that of your children if you have them – as well as the financial impact.

ARE YOU READY?

I have divided the book into chapters. You may find sections, words and phrases that don't relate to your situation, and that's okay just move or phrase it in a way you can relate to it.

I have included a section at the back to help you with divorcing emotionally.

You may be drawn to looking at that first or referring to it as you work through each section.

You might find you turn a page and find something else that needs doing, perhaps washing the kitchen floor or phoning a friend. Stop and ask yourself what you are finding uncomfortable. Look around you and check you are safe. Take a deep breath, thank yourself for making sure your well-being is okay and see what you can complete of the section.

Remember to be honest and raw and not worry about your grammar or spelling.

I have included a bullet journal section in the book. Information can get lost, if you have an idea or find some information, reference the page number and what is on that page in BULLET JOURNAL INDEX.

At the back of the book, I have included a chapter you can use to collect the information you need and the areas you need to negotiate. There are pages at the end of each section for your notes or questions and everything is numbered for you.

WHAT YOU WILL NEED

This book is not exhaustive, it has been designed to stimulate the thought process and provide a base for what you could consider. It is assumed you will do further research and seek advice as part of your divorce process.

- ☐ Grounding Meditation
- ☐ Water
- ☐ Pen and Paper
- ☐ Breathing Technique
- ☐ Goal

You might find resistance with some or all the subjects. Have a few exercises that will help to keep you focused!

Before you start, consider:

- How long you think it will take you

- What will you do if you get stuck or get caught in a flashback or rumination

- How you will break the cycle

Find some meditations to help you.

Search for music, meditations, books and YouTube videos that are helpful and put the links or names below.

You might find a playlist that uplifts you or a YouTube video that affirms your experiences when you wobble.

Keep grounding yourself and breathing. You will find exercises for these at the back.

e.g. STOP the Rumination NOW! https://youtu.be/-8B-jWjHEt8

"

Grief, I've learned, is really just love. It's all the love you want to give, but cannot. All that unspent love gathers up in the corners of your eyes, the lump in your throat, and in that hollow part of your chest. Grief is just love with no place to go.

- Jamie Anderson

"

BULLET JOURNAL INDEX PAGE

Use the following pages to help you find information. For example, you might write something useful for your legal team to know. Look at the page number, then record it in the index below with a reference to the information.

"

Just like an egg: "If an egg
is broken by an outside
force, life ends. If broken by
an inside force, life begins.
Great things always begin
from the inside." Real change
can only come from within.

- Unknown

"

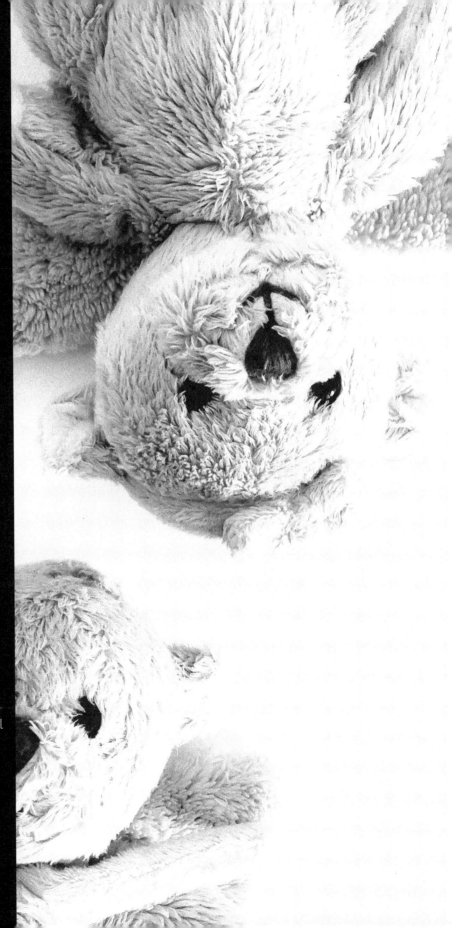

Children

You might find resistance with some or all the subjects. Have a few exercises that will help to keep you focused!

You have a duty of care towards your children.

Children are often used as a secondary source of supply to the emotional abuser, and they can also be used in a smear campaign.

Everything you prepare here will help create a future for them. Consider adding in a clause to renegotiate terms should that be needed.

Your child's needs change, and what is appropriate for a younger child may not be for a teenager. By inserting age triggers, you allow the opportunity to open up a conversation to renegotiate the terms on behalf of your children.

When a company awards a large contract to a supplier, it has an expiry date, and as the contract comes up for renewal, both sides can look at costs and renegotiate. This agreement should be no different.

You may not need to use these triggers; however it will be easier to open up a conversation and renegotiate when these dates arrive rather than trying to approach someone who will use every opportunity to create chaos.

Children change so much. If your children are under five years old, you might want to look at the agreement every six or 12 months. As they get older, you might check this yearly or every three years.

Research apps or platforms that could help you communicate.

By divorcing emotionally, you will be in a better position to set and enforce boundaries keeping the focus on your children.

These are your negotiations. Do what feels right for you, not what everyone else is doing or what your legal team suggests.

Change your mindset and view this as a contract negotiation.

> If you need more space for the answers, use a notebook. You can also use it to journal how you feel about each question. Visualise what your life looks and feels like in the future.

CHILDREN

Use this section to 'inner-stand' what is important to you and your children. Have you agreed on child custody, visitation, living arrangements, and support? What would be the ideal scenario for you?

Ideal scenario

Next best scenario

Have you agreed on responsibilities for health care for the children? Have you discussed who pays additional costs or how you divide medical costs which may not be covered? What would be the ideal scenario for you? Include dentistry and eye care.

Possible expenses

Who will be responsible?

Consider if there is a change in circumstances

Ideal scenario

Next best scenario

What would you do in the situation where one parent wanted a medical procedure and the other didn't?

Ideal scenario

Next best scenario

What are the costs of nursery or childcare? What are the costs for children's activities and school trips or camps? Evening groups or weekend activities? Consider any costs for uniforms or special clothing, and clothing for trips in addition to everyday needs. Also, consider the cost of childcare for working parents during the school holidays. How will the costs be allocated?

Have you agreed on ground rules for leaving children alone at home? Technology usage? Food? Anything else?

Have you agreed on ground rules for meeting potential new romantic interests in each of your lives? What time frame is acceptable to you? What contact with the children is acceptable to you? Would you want to meet the person before they met your children? Do you require any special background checks to be made?

In your view, what would the ideal scenario be?

Would you consider putting in a caveat to this agreement? What would happen if you or your ex were to remarry within this time frame? Would the trigger be an engagement, or leading up to a wedding? Remember, not all engagements make it down the aisle.

Would you consider a caveat?

Have you built safeguards on how to make decisions in the future? Have you considered how you raise concerns?

Ideal scenario

Next best scenario

Have you considered how disagreements will be handled?

What events and dates do you want to negotiate? Consider summer holidays, birthdays, Mother's Day, Father's Day and important family events or gatherings.

Plan for future events where either of you has a wedding to attend or holidays you have been invited on. How will you discuss this, and what can you put in place here that helps with future negotiations?

Your children change, and so do their needs. What works for them as young children won't necessarily as teenagers. You might get to the date, and everything is working. Think about putting dates that this agreement will get renegotiated and how this will happen. Would you like to check every year or every other year – or perhaps at the eldest child's birthday?

What will you need to do to make this happen?

Use this space to consider where your ex might disagree with any or all of the questions or ideas.

Consider:

- Custody, visitation, living arrangements, support, additional medical costs, and agreements for a medical procedure.
- Childcare costs, after-school activities, clothing, activities, groups, and costs of special clothing.

- Ground rules, leaving children unsupervised, technology, food.
- Meeting partners, caveat agreement.
- Dates for holidays, birthdays and special events.
- Disagreements.

Is there anything else you would add? What ideas do you have?

As you went through this section, did it bring up any fears?

During your research what apps, platforms and support groups do you think would be useful?

"

Hold yourself back, or
heal yourself back
together. You decide.

- Brittany Burgunder

"

SPOUSAL SUPPORT

This workbook is not exhaustive. It has been designed to stimulate the thought process and provide a base for what you could consider. And it is assumed you will do further research and seek advice as part of your divorce process.

Everything you do here will help create your future.

If you can Emotionally Divorce before you start the negotiations, it will help you see the circumstances differently and set boundaries.

When you start looking at finances, make a list of your expenditure. Once you have done that, create a list of what you expect to see on the other party's expenditure sheet. Included at the back of this book is a list you can use to help with your financial planning, as well as a guide to check the other party's planning.

When you receive the other side's financials, work through them line by line. Highlight anything you believe is missing. If the expenditure is higher than their income, this could indicate another source of income or an additional bank account.

You may have honed your detective skills during the relationship. Put this new talent to good use here. Check that their payslips are consistent: are there any missing? What bank accounts do you remember them having when you were married?

Have they taken out any credit cards in your name or against your address?

What about loans or lease agreements?

If you are told that accounts have been closed, request confirmation of this.

> Be honest about your needs. Divorce emotionally, and you will not be manipulated by them and their ridiculous claims, the smear campaign and their victim story.

SPOUSAL SUPPORT

Use this section for what is important to you and your future.

Have you reached an agreement on spousal support?

Have you come to a financial agreement?

Have you considered how long this support will be for? How often will it be reviewed? What will be the triggers for review?

Do you have a system built into your agreement to address future conflicts?

Do you feel that you have a thorough understanding of how the agreement was reached? And how the agreement will affect you financially and emotionally in the future?

Do you feel that your ex has a thorough understanding of how the agreement was reached? And how the agreement will affect you financially and emotionally in the future?

Ideal scenario

Next best scenario

How clear are you on money?

Do you have shares, stocks, bonds, or bitcoin? Do you know what your ex earned? Do you know of any offshore accounts? Who did you bank with? Do you still have a joint account?

Use this space to write down the information you recall - keep coming back as you remember things.

Use this space to consider where your ex might disagree with any or all of the questions or ideas.

Spousal support, the financial agreement, reviews, stocks, shares, bitcoin and pension splits.

Do you have a strategy if your ex isn't able to pay you or stops paying you? How confident are you that your ex intends to adhere to the agreement?

Can you build in a clause that addresses what happens in the event of your ex not adhering to the agreement?

Is there anything else you would add in? What ideas has it given you? You can keep coming back to this section as the ideas flow.

As you went through this section, what fears did it bring up?

"

There is a stillness in me. It is deeper than grief. I am wondering why, when I call home, everything seems to be happening as usual. Yes life must go on. But I wonder when the healing will begin, when we will stop laughing to hide the pain?

- Yvonne Weekes, Volcano

"

ASSETS

This workbook is not exhaustive. It has been designed to stimulate the thought process and provide a base for what you could consider. And it is assumed you will do further research and seek advice as part of your divorce process.

As with the spousal support exercise, everything you do here will help create your future. By divorcing emotionally, you see your worth. It will help you set boundaries and ask for what you want.

When you start considering the assets, list everything – not just the items you would like. This will help you with your negotiation.

You may discover that they have an attitude of 'what is yours is mine, and what is mine is mine'.

It is very likely that the negotiation has taken place in their head, and they have decided what you are worth, which creates for them a possible attitude of 'you will pay for this'.

Those promises of 'giving you everything' have changed to 'make you pay.'

Being divorced emotionally will help you determine how much an item is worth fighting for and how much you are willing to pay in time, energy and money. It will help you consider how you feel about it and what it means to you. Will you be staring at a picture in a few years, hating the item, as it reminds you of the divorce or relationship?

Don't just list the items you would like. Write down everything as it will help you with your negotiation.

ASSETS

Use this section to 'inner-stand' what is important to you and your future. Have you reached an agreement on dividing assets? The marital home, motor vehicles, holiday homes, etc.?

Ideal scenario

Next best scenario

Have decisions been made of who will create the division?

Has a time frame been set for this to happen?

How will this be communicated?

What information will you require to confirm that the division or transfer has been made or the names have been changed on contracts?

Ideal scenario

Next best scenario

Have you reached an agreement on the distribution of liabilities, such as credit cards, debt and mortgages? List your liabilities below.

Consider:

- Has a time frame been set for this to happen?
- How will this be communicated?
- What information will you require to confirm the division or transfer has been made or the names have been changed on contracts?

Ideal scenario

Next best scenario

Have you agreed on the division of retirement assets, and have you made these decisions understanding the full financial and tax implications for both parties?

Retirement Assets

Financial and Tax Implications

Need to know

Policy Information, held with, value, policy dates

Have you discussed health insurance?

Have you agreed on what rights you will maintain in regard to each other's life insurance policies? Or if a new one will need to be drawn up?

Do you feel that you understand your ex-partner's finances? What do you need to know? Are there any discrepancies?

Finances

Need to know

Discrepancies

Do you believe your ex has a full and accurate understanding of your finances?

Have you agreed to a division of personal effects, household goods, and furnishings? Use the boxes to grade each item of importance to you personally.

List your assets. In **COLUMN A**, put the things that are non-negotiable for you. Use **COLUMN B** for the things you might be willing to give up or negotiate on. **COLUMN C** is for everything that you are happy for them to win. This list is for your eyes only.

A. Non-negotiable	B. Important, but negotiable	C. Important to them

A. Non-negotiable

B. Important, but negotiable

C. Important to them

A. Non-negotiable

B. Important, but negotiable

C. Important to them

What would you like more information on?

Use this space to consider where your ex might disagree with any or all of the questions or ideas.

Consider:

- Marital home
- Motor vehicles
- Holiday homes
- Credit cards
- Debt and mortgages
- Retirement assets

- Tax implications
- Health insurance
- Life insurance
- Personal effects
- Household goods and furnishings

As you went through this section, what fears did it bring up?

Is there anything else you would add? What ideas has it given you?

There is complete silence around her, but I can feel her heart breaking. It is being cracked open and I can hear a silent sobbing coming from deep inside her, but for an outsider, you wouldn't know that, you can't hear it.

- Elizabeth Goddard • Finding Lily

COST OF DIVORCE

This workbook is not exhaustive. It has been designed to stimulate the thought process and provide a base for what you could consider. And it is assumed you will do further research and seek advice as part of your divorce process.

What is the real cost?

If you managed to get out of the relationship with your soul intact, you are lucky!

The emotions you might experience might be like riding a rollercoaster.

From out of nowhere, you might find tears rolling down your face, and in the next moment, you are overcome with anger.

Make sure you fully understand what you are agreeing to.

You might hear statements like 'we can sort this out ourselves' or 'you don't need legal assistance'.

If you allow them to divorce you in exchange for a payment, what does that entail? Consider what is involved and the claims they could make about your character.

If you need more space, get a notebook or paper. You can also journal on how you feel about each question and visualise how this looks and feels in the future.

COST OF DIVORCE

Use this section for what is important to you and important to your future. Have you agreed on how to cover the costs of divorce? (Legal fees, filing fees, court fees, etc.).

Use this space to consider where your ex might disagree with any or all of the questions or ideas.

Consider:

- Legal fees
- Filing fees
- Court fees, etc

As you went through this section, what fears did it bring up?

Is there anything else you need to consider? What ideas has it given you?

Consider the real cost

Consider the real cost of divorce when you're negotiating every area. Tune into your body and check in with who is running it: you, or a wound?

When completing the division of assets, ask yourself how important an item is.

There is nothing worse than spending time and money on an item that once the divorce is over, you can't bear to look at.

Also, consider what items you have available to negotiate with. What is important to you that might just become the most important item to your ex?

Take photographs of items, and document everything.

Is there anything else you would add? What ideas has it given you? You can keep coming back to this section as the ideas flow.

134

Trauma is a fact of life. It does not, however, have to be a life sentence.

- Peter A. Levine

EMOTIONAL ISSUES

This workbook is not exhaustive. It has been designed to stimulate the thought process and provide a base for what you could consider. And it is assumed you will do further research and seek advice as part of your divorce process.

Being divorced emotionally will help you determine how much an item is worth fighting for, and how much you are willing to pay in time, energy and money. It will help you consider how you feel about it and what it means to you. Will you be staring at a picture in a few years, hating it, as it reminds you of the divorce or relationship?

Emotional divorce will ensure your wounds are not running your divorce.

Use this section to fully inner-stand what you want from this process. If you can, reframe your thoughts and view this as a contract for the next part of your life.

Think about the real cost of your divorce. I am not talking about the financial cost – this section is about the emotional cost to you and your family.

If you manage to get out with your soul intact, you were lucky!

You might experience a rollercoaster of emotions. If you can divorce emotionally, the divorce is then being driven by what is best for you and you will not be manipulated.

Your decisions will be from what is best for you and your future. And divorcing emotionally will help you set strong boundaries for the future.

If you need more space, get a notebook or paper. You can also journal on how you feel about each question and visualise how this looks and feels in the future.

EMOTIONAL ISSUES

Do you and your ex have mechanisms built into your agreement to address any future conflict that may arise between the two of you?

Do you feel that you have a thorough understanding of how the agreement has been reached and how it will affect you financially and emotionally in the future?

Do you feel that either one of you made decisions out of anger, shock or denial?

Do you believe your ex understands these agreements and intends to adhere to them?

Use this space to consider where your ex might disagree with any or all of the questions or ideas.

Consider:

- Children
- Spousal support
- Assets
- Cost of divorce

As you went through this section, what fears did it bring up? Is there anything else you would add? What ideas has it given you?

66

Trauma Is Not What
Happens to You, It Is What
Happens Inside You

- Gabor Mate

99

CHECKLIST

What do you need to put in place?

Children

- [ ]
- [ ]
- [ ]
- [ ]
- [ ]
- [ ]
- [ ]
- [ ]

Spousal Support

- [ ]
- [ ]
- [ ]
- [ ]
- [ ]
- [ ]
- [ ]
- [ ]

Assets

- [ ]
- [ ]
- [ ]
- [ ]
- [ ]
- [ ]
- [ ]
- [ ]

Costs

- [ ]
- [ ]
- [ ]
- [ ]
- [ ]
- [ ]
- [ ]
- [ ]

Emotional Issues

- [ ]
- [ ]
- [ ]
- [ ]
- [ ]
- [ ]
- [ ]
- [ ]

Other

- [ ]
- [ ]
- [ ]
- [ ]
- [ ]
- [ ]
- [ ]
- [ ]

Financial Overview			
Total of ALL monthly income		Total of ALL monthly outgoings	
Amount left over			
Home & Contents			
Mortgage/Rent		Ground Rent and Service Charges	
Council Tax		Secured Loans	
Mortgage Endowment		Household Appliance Hire/ Purchase	
Help to Buy Loan			
Utilities			
Gas		Duel Fuel	
Electricity		Other Fuel	
Water			
Care & Health Costs			
Prescriptions and Medicine		Opticians	
Dentistry		Child Maintenance or Support	
Childcare		Adult Care or Support	

Transport & Travel			
Car Insurance		Breakdown Cover	
Road Tax		MOT Vehicle Maintenance	
Fuel, Parking and Toll Road Charges		Vehicle Lease	
Loan		Public Transport	
Pensions & Insurances			
Buildings Insurance		Mortgage Protection Insurance	
Home Contents Insurance		Health Insurance	
Life Insurance		Pension	
Pet Insurance			
Professional Costs			
Professional Courses		Professional Fees	
Union Fees			
School Charges			
School Uniform		Breakfast and After School Clubs	
School Fees		School Trips	
Books and Resources		Extra Tuition	

Other Costs			
Fines		Loan from friend or family member	
Legal Fees			
Food & Housekeeping			
Groceries		Food at Work	
Alcohol		Smoking Prooducts	
Laundry and Dry Cleaning		Household Repairs and Maintenance	
Nappies and Baby Items		School Meals	
Pet Food		Vet Bills	
Telephone & Entertainment			
Home Phone, Internet and TV Package		Mobile Phone	
TV Subscription		Hobbies, Leisure or Sport	
Newspapers, Magazines, Stationery and Postage		Donations	
TV Licence			

Personal Costs			
Clothing		Children's Clothing	
Toiletries		Hair and Makeup	
Nails		Children's Allowance	
Gifts			

Income			
Wages		Other Earnings	
State Allowance		Child Support	
Other Benefits		Pension	
Other Income			

"The first morning passed, and the first afternoon, then the first shift back at work. Time takes it all, whether you want it to or not. Time takes it all, time bears it away, and in the end there is only darkness. Sometimes we find others in that darkness, and sometimes we lose them there again."

- Stephen King

Divorce matters for your wellbeing. It is an important process which can get hijacked, but if you can get the closure you need and heal the emotional wounds, you can move forward and claim back the power and control of your own life.

Your divorce matters are very important as well: this might be the only chance you get to ask for the information you need. Take the opportunity to dot all the i's and cross all the t's and start to create the life you deserve to live.

- Elizabeth Goddard

Divorce Matters

A practical guide to Support your
Healing Journey.

ELIZABETH GODDARD

You do not have to relive any of it; there are ways to release pain and trauma effectively.

I have included this section to help you divorce emotionally from the abuser.

When the relationship is over you can get stuck in your head, going over every scenario and wondering what they are up to now.

Three very simple tools (although there are more in this section) are grounding, breathing and honest conversations.

Being in your body is so very important when you are recovering. The gaslighting that took place convinced you that what you thought was true was a lie and what was a lie was the truth. This is your very own Alice through the looking glass moment. *The phrase[1] 'Through the Looking Glass' can be viewed as a metaphor for any time the world suddenly appears unfamiliar, almost as if things were turned upside down. – similar to looking out from inside the mirror to find a world both recognizable and yet turned inside-out.*

Grounding and breathing are very quick ways of stopping the thoughts in their tracks before you lose days and weeks to rumination.

Coming out of these relationships you have more questions than answers and easily slip into rumination which is the process of continuously thinking about the same thoughts, which tend to be sad or dark. Rumination can be dangerous to your mental health, it prolongs your ability to think and process emotions.

By grounding into your body you stay out of your head which helps you process what has happened and what is happening to you. Breathing and counting also help you be in your body whilst balancing the stress hormones and calming down your nervous system.

I have come to the conclusion that human beings
are born with an innate capacity to triumph over
trauma. I believe not only that trauma is curable,
but that the healing process can be a catalyst
for profound awakening - a portal opening to
emotional and genuine spiritual transformation.
I have little doubt that as individuals, families,
communities, and even nations, we have the
capacity to learn how to heal and prevent much
of the damage done by trauma. In so doing, we
will significantly increase our ability to achieve
both our individual and collective dreams.

- Peter A. Levine

BREAKING THE TRAUMA BOND.

When you realise the outcome really wouldn't have changed if you had said or done anything differently, and that CLOSURE isn't something you would ever get from the abuser, you are there. By breaking the trauma bond and giving yourself the closure you need, you can divorce emotionally.

Breaking the bond is a process that works for you and your needs. There isn't a step-by-step guide. But you will find these useful in breaking it.

Write out your story

This is an important part of the process, and it will stop you from getting trapped in rumination.

When you start to question if you are doing the right thing or if this is all your fault, you can refer back to the story.

Grounding and Breathing

When coming out of this type of relationship, it is common to live in your head. Your mind has been tricked, and the gaslighting that took place has you questioning everything.

Grounding and Breathing will help you to stay in your body, and from there you can gain more clarity and be honest with yourself about what has happened, rather than excuse their behaviour. You know you are healing the wounds and breaking the bonds.

Honest conversations

If you are still overcome with emotions, wanting them back, turn inwards and have an honest conversation with yourself. What do you really want?

WRITING THE STORY...

The power of words is so, so healing.

Use your story to understand what happened. Writing your story will also help you in the moments when you doubt yourself and when you are ruminating, believing this is all your fault. Your story, along with other tools, will remind you of what happened. It will remind you of the manipulation and coercive control that took place, and it will help you if it continues during the divorce process.

With a pen and a notebook, write it out by hand, which I believe is so powerful (I believe there is a direct connection between the hand and mind, you can write and draw out your emotions and heal and process quicker than typing them out). It can be in any order: you can start at the beginning or in the middle. What memory is coming up for you?

Once you have written your story, go back through it and see if you can identify any manipulative behaviour that took place.

GROUNDING

You can search for guided meditations that will help you to ground.

A simple exercise is to focus on your stomach area just below your rib cage. Imagine a cord of light appears there and then travels down your body and splits in two, travelling down each leg. See the light travel out of your feet and into the earth, travelling to the centre and anchoring itself at the core. Return your focus to the centre of your body again and see the cord going upwards through your body and out of the crown of your head. Watch the light travel up through the sky and through the clouds and head towards the sun or the moon, where it anchors itself to whichever one you select. Allow the energy of the earth and the energy of the sun or moon to filter through the cords and charge you, keeping you anchored in your body.

An alternative to this is when the cord comes out of your feet, you can see it spread out like the roots of a tree, creating a solid bond and earthing you.

Please do not do this whilst driving or operating machinery.

Consider building this into your morning routine, perhaps whilst cleaning your teeth or while you wait for the kettle to boil.

BREATHING

You can search for breathing meditations that will help you.

A simple exercise is to take a deep breath in counting to your favourite number - I use 6.

You then hold your breath for the same count.

Release your breath to the same number and hold it again for the same count and you repeat this process for a few minutes or longer or until you feel calmer.

An alternative to this is using a phrase or statement. 'I am supported in this process' or 'I release the trauma held in my body' or perhaps 'I am loved, I am love, I am free'.

Each stage must be the same length, and it is particularly helpful in the event you get trapped in a cycle of rumination.

Please do not do this whilst driving or operating machinery.

Consider building this into your morning routine, perhaps whilst cleaning your teeth or while you wait for the kettle to boil.

HONEST CONVERSATIONS

There will be moments when you want to reach out. You may have seen a glimpse of the person you thought they were or you just think you need them.

The only person you can be really honest with is yourself. You may have a counsellor or therapist, but it takes time to build trust. And, let's be honest: will you truly share everything with them?

We have three core emotions: abandonment, shame, and betrayal, and you may have experienced all of them. You may discuss your emotions, but you hold back certain things for fear of being judged or the shame you are experiencing.

Remember, the one person you can be honest with is yourself.

Ask yourself what you really need: is it attention, or do you really want or need the abuser?

Sit quietly and ask what you need. Feel where the pain is in the body and talk to it. You may be surprised what the answer is.

It might be a hug or just to be heard.

Maybe you want to scream or cry.

This technique is really powerful, and will save you a lot of time, money and wasted energy. It will help you break the bonds and get closure. There is a damaged inner child that craves the attention it was given, and you can fulfil that role yourself.

Please do not do this whilst driving or operating machinery.

WHEN YOU GET STUCK

When you get stuck, get out your pen and write out what happened. Then take a step back and read this as if it were written by your best friend.

Read it through and then answer as you would to them.

MONEY MONEY MONEY MONEY

One of the quickest ways for an abuser to control you is financially. It stops you from walking away and abandoning them, and they also have this weird obsession with money (in my experience).

You might have come out of this relationship broke as well as broken.

They couldn't contribute to, or pay, bills or the mortgage or rent because they had a huge bill to pay, or they claimed they needed their money for something else.

And yet, they are so generous towards other people. They find relationships boring; they play the game of dutiful husband or wife but it holds nothing for them apart from being a mask to hide behind.

What I would like you to do is to think about the times they were generous. Then recall the times they didn't have the money to pay, forcing you to use your money.

You may walk away with nothing or with huge debts, while they, on the other hand, move on to a new life, debt-free and in a far better position financially.

Going into the divorce process, you need to sit down and start looking at what you want. By divorcing emotionally, you can start thinking about what you actually want your life to look like. It might be that you have two professionals assisting you: one for the divorce process and one for you.

The abuser has already decided your worth. They want to win at any cost, and they really do not care by how little – as long as they win. And part of this win is to make you pay in some way: it might be monetary, but it might be with your mind or soul. You are not a person to them; you are an object. That is why they were able to walk away from you without a backward glance and move on, leaving you to clear up their mess.

As an object, you hold no value to them, but they understand that the divorce process does hold value. Relationships with the emotional abuser are projects: they studied you from the very beginning, so they know exactly what they need to do and say to hurt you.

LET'S TALK TALK

The conversations you have with yourself will be the most powerful.

You can speak to a counsellor or therapist, and it can be very helpful initially, but it doesn't go deep enough and you might not be as honest with them as you might be with yourself.

I believe that healing THE ORIGINAL WOUND is crucial to living the life you know deep down you were meant to live.

Remember, the decisions you make will affect the people looking up to you: your children, or the people around you, are learning from you. If you have children, you are telling them it is okay to be treated the way you have.

You are a ripple in this world. It may not feel like this will have a huge impact on anyone, but think of the butterfly effect. The decisions you make now will have an impact on someone, somewhere in the world.

In the moments where you miss the abuser or you believe this is all your fault, ask yourself what you really need,

The truth is, by hiding the pain and pretending you are okay, you are just burying the emotion until it comes up again and again and again.

Over time I hope you will see this as a GIFT.

You will learn that no one can understand your needs, as well as you. By not addressing THE ORIGINAL WOUND, you are at risk of repeating the pattern and prolonging your recovery

By taking RESPONSIBILITY for the role you played and finding THE ORIGINAL WOUND, this allows you to heal and feel whole,

THAT is the GIFT.

It allows you to take back control and realise you can't heal them – that is their job.

By taking ownership of your life, you are now responsible for your energy, your thoughts, and your healing. Taking ownership of your feelings means you are taking responsibility for your life. You start to live in the present, not in the past, and you will begin to realise how much quicker you are getting out of your negative thought patterns and how quickly your emotions are changing.

It is crucial to acknowledge your journey: to acknowledge who you were before the relationship, who you were during the relationship, and who you are now, even if you feel your life is a mess. You can acknowledge each step of the journey. It is going to be fierce and painful, and your other alternative is to go back to the relationship. BUT please remember, you are going to have to go through this at some point in the future.

HELLO, CAN YOU HEAR ME?

NO CONTACT is a powerful way to start the healing process. If no contact is not an option, grey rock is. Become as interesting as a GREY ROCK.

Find a rock and study it; ask it some questions:

How is it?
What is its favourite place to stay?
What about its favourite weather conditions?
Did you get a reply?

That is exactly how to behave: you become as interesting as a grey rock. You can smile when you say 'I am very well, thank you very much'. You don't engage in conversation, and you don't ask how they are.

You can do a handover with them for the children or dog, but that is where it ends. If you are asked if you have plans for the weekend, you might say I haven't thought about it. If you are asked about your friends and family, reply with 'they are well, thank you'. Don't mention the illness or wedding or the holiday you are planning.

Start changing how you view the relationship; this is a contract you have with them. If you were drawing up a contract with a supplier, how would you view them asking for your personal details?

Go outside and find a grey rock and have a conversation with it. It doesn't have to be grey, it could be white or brown or black for the purpose of this exercise. A rock is a rock. I appreciate a geologist might disagree and will explain the information the rock holds, but it doesn't verbally talk and if it did, it wouldn't talk about the weekend it has planned.

Being emotionally divorced means you can hear their name and feel nothing, you can receive an email and feel nothing, and you can get a message and feel nothing. Every wound they created has been healed (or the ones they triggered), and the invisible bonds are severed.

The abuser knows your triggers, and they know how to execute them for their pleasure. When they say they don't want to fight, they just want to move on, what they really mean is they don't want you to fight them. When you divorce emotionally, you are in a stronger position to say no!

You are in a stronger position to make decisions that suit your agenda, not theirs.
You are in a stronger position to get the divorce that works for you.
You are in a stronger position to spot the manipulation.
You are in a stronger position to walk away if you so choose.

Divorce emotionally first. If you are stuck in the trauma bond, you will still remember the persona they created at the beginning of the relationship, the one who was so kind and loving towards you and you might believe that they want to protect you.

Trust your intuition.

Check in with yourself and ask how you feel and also if this is really what you want.

SO, TO SUMMARISE....

If you feel something is wrong, then it probably is – despite them trying to make you believe this is your fault.

You might find it helpful to write out your story and see the patterns. Remember, you know more than you think you do.

You may have caught them cheating. They will apologise and beg your forgiveness; they may have promised to change, but they didn't – they have learnt to disguise it better.

They may have promised you everything and said they wouldn't fight you for anything.

You saw the way they treated others, but you believed them when they told you that you were the only one who understood them. Be prepared to be treated the same way.

They never take responsibility and always play the VICTIM. Look at the patterns and ask yourself who is the common denominator.

You may discover that your money is their money, and their money is their own. This is COERCIVE CONTROL.

A TO Z

OF EMOTIONAL ABUSE

This is an excerpt from The A-Z of EMOTIONAL ABUSE.

The book describes the words you hear as you enter this new place of learning and healing.

I have taken a few words used in the book to help you understand some of the techniques that were used to control and manipulate you.

Revive Your Soul Publishing;
Illustrated edition
(14 Feb. 2020)
SBN-13 : 978-1916357709

ABUSE · The definition of ABUSE is to use something to bad effect or for a bad purpose, such as the ABUSE of alcohol and drugs. Abuse is to assault someone or treat them in such a way as to cause damage or harm, or to speak to someone in an insulting and offensive way.

ABUSIVE CYCLES · The ongoing rotation of destructive behaviour used to gain power and control over a person. The CYCLE OF ABUSE is idealisation, devaluation, discard.

At the very beginning of the relationship, everything you said and did was watched and noted. They swept you off your feet with compliments, gifts, days and meals out. Your every need was catered for, and this was deliberate.

The messages they sent early in the morning ensured they were the first thing you thought about, and again at the end of the day, so you went to bed thinking about them. It allowed them to MANUFACTURE a relationship where you had so much in common: you shared the same hopes and dreams and had the same insecurities. They told you that no one had ever understood them, and you were SOULMATES.

The ABUSER used the devaluation STAGE to make sure you were more invested in protecting the relationship than you were in protecting yourself. They did this by making comments about your intelligence or your abilities and perhaps your goals and dreams. If you QUESTIONED them, they might have told you that you were being oversensitive, or they were only joking!   These BELITTLING comments and subtle put-downs were followed by idealisation, which changed the chemicals in your body. You found yourself addicted, and you over-rode your INTUITION. They used techniques such as TRIANGULATION that made them look popular, MANUFACTURING situations to make you feel JEALOUS and QUESTION their fidelity.

You may have experienced GASLIGHTING, where they convinced you that what you were feeling wasn't real, or that you didn't understand the situation or your facts were wrong. And they were so believable, you actually QUESTIONED yourself.

Following the devaluation stage, the ABUSER tested you by discarding you in some way. They did this to make sure you were BONDED to them. They might have disappeared, and you were unable to get hold of them. They then reappeared with a gift or compliment, giving you back the feeling you had at the beginning of the relationship and reaffirming that they did love you! You had noticed the cracks in their mask, but you justified their actions because they kept reaffirming their love for you by taking you back to the love bombing stage again and again and again.

BOUNDARIES · The definition of a BOUNDARY is a line which marks an area, a dividing line. We understand the BOUNDARY that surrounds a property to mark an area. Personal BOUNDARIES are the same, they are the limits we create to keep us safe and the way we will allow other people to behave towards us.

The EMOTIONAL ABUSER perceived your BOUNDARIES during the idealisation stage, and they very slowly broke them down. They started by pushing against them to see how far they could go and what they could get away with.

You may have told them you weren't happy about their behaviour, and they apologised but continued. It is done so subtly that you don't realise this is what they are doing. No means no: it doesn't mean maybe.

CLOSURE · Relationship CLOSURE involves honest, healthy, non-judgmental communication that helps with letting go. Being denied CLOSURE when you're breaking up is unhealthy: it's damaging, destructive and controlling. Relationships break down for different reasons. Healthy people are able to acknowledge what isn't working; it can be painful, but CLOSURE is helpful in moving on for both parties. But this wasn't a healthy relationship!

There are a few reasons you are denied closure. Firstly, they play the VICTIM: the attention they receive from their friends, family, work colleagues or the person next to them on the train SUPPLIES them. Why would they give that up? Secondly, seeing you in pain is SUPPLYING them with attention, they don't care if it is negative or positive – it's SUPPLY!

Knowing that they have caused this pain is the proof they need to show how powerful they are and reinforces the amount of control they still have over you.

COERCIVE CONTROL · is described as an act or a pattern of assault carried out through forms of threats, humiliation and intimidation.

COERCIVE CONTROL is EMOTIONAL ABUSE, it is used to harm, punish and frighten the VICTIM.

This form of behaviour is used to make the VICTIM dependent on the ABUSER. ISOLATING them from friends and family, they exploit them and deprive them of their independence, and regulate their everyday behaviour. COERCIVE or controlling behaviour does not relate to one single incident; it is a pattern that occurs over time. It is used for one individual to exert power and control over another.

COERCIVE CONTROL creates invisible chains. People might ask why you didn't leave earlier, or why you didn't see what was going on.

Some common examples of COERCIVE behaviour are[2]:

- ISOLATING you from friends and family, monitoring your time
- Monitoring you via online communication tools or spyware
- Taking CONTROL over aspects of your everyday life, such as where you can go, whom you can see, what you can wear and when you can sleep
- Depriving you of access to support services, such as medical services
- Repeatedly putting you down, such as saying you're worthless
- Humiliating, degrading or dehumanising you
- CONTROLLING your finances
- Making threats or intimidating you

COGNITIVE DISSONANCE · Occurs when we experience a state of holding two or more contradictory thoughts or beliefs at the same time.

In a relationship, this can be the belief that your partner loves you, but you are experiencing conflict when their behaviour doesn't MIRROR their words.

COGNITIVE DISSONANCE, or GASLIGHTING, is a very unique experience for each individual. Only a person who has gone through this very specific form of ABUSE will understand what it is like, and how deep the trauma runs.

This form of ABUSE penetrates so many levels, so many layers; your brain has been tricked to believe what you were told was the truth, it takes time to de-traumatise. And it is so easy to slip back down the dark hole when faced with new facts and new situations.

EMOTIONAL ABUSE · A pattern of behaviour: one person uses fear, humiliation, guilt or manipulation tactics to gain power over another.

Unlike physical ABUSE, it often goes unnoticed, and the damage it causes puts you into a state of confusion. You had no idea it was taking place; and like Chinese water torture, it happened very slowly and turned you crazy. They chipped away at your Self-esteem, and you began to doubt your perceptions and reality.

EMOTIONAL DIVORCE · The key is divorcing emotionally from the abuse; it means breaking the trauma bonds, and getting the closure you deserve and it means giving no fucks. When the abuser reaches out in an attempt to hoover you, saying they are so sorry and they have now realised what you had together, or they attempt to trigger a reaction from you, you feel nothing.

When you divorce emotionally, you don't react to their drama or manipulation tactics.

Your reaction allows them to wear a mask and play the victim. Divorcing them emotionally will mean that they will not get what they want.

FUTURE FAKING · The future you created together was manufactured during the idealisation stage. They listened to your every word and watched your every move, possibly stalking your social media accounts. Nothing about that future was real, but the stories around it were so believable. They took just enough of your dreams for the future, which they intertwined into THE FAKE FUTURE they created with you, so you believed they were as invested in the relationship as you were.

GASLIGHTING · A covert way of distorting another person's perception of reality; making them question their sanity and their memory. This is Crazy-Making; it makes you think that you're actually going CRAY, CRAY (craziness at a whole different level).

You can't trust yourself, or your perception of reality.

You start to believe the Abuser's version of events, and slowly they begin to take over your life.

Gaslighting was used to make you feel something was wrong with you. They used tactics to deflect from their behaviour, making you feel you were mentally unstable, or that you were overreacting.

For people healing from these TOXIC relationships, this can cause emotional confusion and anxiety.

Eventually, you may have started to wonder what was happening, and felt that you couldn't trust your own judgement.

Gaslighting is really dangerous, creating feelings of insecurity, confusion, brain fog, self-doubt, fear, not feeling good enough and feeling vulnerable or powerless.

GREY ROCK · A technique that can be used when you aren't able to do NO CONTACT, it might be because you share children with your abuser, or the person may be a family member or work colleague.

Become as interesting as a GREY ROCK. Stop being a source of SUPPLY for their drama and attention; they will become bored and move on.

Use neutral language and tone; if you need to have a conversation, talk about boring subjects. Do not reveal anything going on in your life. Think of the most boring character you know, take on their persona and play that role. Do not engage with them on any level, especially emotionally. Use YES and NO answers, and don't make any effort for them; as well as not being interesting with your language, you can take it further with your appearance, by wearing plain and simple or slouchy clothing. By divorcing emotionally the need to run to the wardrobe and find your heels or that shirt they loved you in, to show them what they are missing is gone.

HOOVERING · The term used to describe being "sucked back in" following a discard. Just like a vacuum cleaner, the ABUSER attempts to get you back.

You might have been hoovered when you started to see who they really were, and what was going on. Or maybe you were questioning their behaviour, realising it wasn't healthy. Perhaps when you were asking for guidance from your friends and family. You might have experienced HOOVERING at the end of the relationship if they sensed you were moving on. They are 'just checking you are okay'. They have realised they can't live without you. They are hurting. They need you. They don't want you going through this alone. And the list goes on.

INNER-STANDING · 'Inner-standing' is the inner knowing; it is your intuition, the unarguable knowledge that something is true.

LOVE BOMBING · Idealisation is also known as LOVE BOMBING.

NARCISSIST · A person who behaves in a selfish way, with a grandiose sense of importance, and an insatiable need for admiration, wealth, power or fame. They lack empathy and consideration for others.

NARCISSISTS feel entitled to special treatment; they are easily offended and readily harbour grudges. However, they are often very popular, until you are no longer of use to them, and they discard you.

They are children in an adult's body, unable to take RESPONSIBILITY for any of their actions, and anyone who disagrees with them or their unreasonable expectations might be subjected to their NARCISSISTIC RAGE. There are seven levels of anger from getting triggered to acting on the anger, but NARCISSISTIC RAGE goes from 0-7 in an instant.

Their unmet needs as a child meant they were unable to master critical emotional development.

Narcissism is a personality disorder which is diagnosed by a mental health professional. It is likely you took the blame for the breakdown of the relationship, so it is unlikely that they would agree to an appointment for a diagnosis.

I refer to the NARCISSIST, sociopath and psychopath as Emotional Abuser or toxic person; narcissists, sociopaths and psychopaths are much higher up on that NARCISSISTIC scale, but it is quite rare that one would get help.

Under the label of NARCISSIST, you will find different types:

- **Overt NARCISSIST** · This is probably the type that jumps to mind. They have a grandiose sense of importance where the world revolves around them.

- **Covert NARCISSIST** · They are as self-absorbed and as destructive in relationships as the overt, but they just aren't as loud and obvious.

- **Cerebral NARCISSIST** · These are the know-it-alls, who use their intellect or knowledge to secure their SUPPLY.

- **Somatic NARCISSIST** · They flaunt their conquests and parade their possessions or show off their muscles.

- **Inverted NARCISSISTS** · They rely on other people for their emotional gratification, and have the tendency to put other people first, looking for relationships that make them feel validated or needed.

NARCISSISTIC SUPPLY · The term used to describe the constant attention that the NARCISSIST needs. This will be from anyone who can provide attention, good or bad.

When you come out of an Emotionally Abusive relationship, it is important you stop providing them with NARCISSISTIC SUPPLY. You can do this by going NO CONTACT. If for any reason you can't do this, then GREY ROCK is a solution.

NO CONTACT · This is a tool you can use to protect yourself and your energy. This means cutting off all forms of communication with a person to protect yourself from recurring trauma, allowing you to heal from the relationship. This means deleting them from all social media, as well as blocking emails and phone contact.

This also means **you** don't look at their social media profiles.

If you have children together, going NO CONTACT might be difficult. Explore any way you can to limit the contact you have with the ABUSER and try using GREY ROCK.

Be careful with mediation. They play the VICTIM so well that you may find yourself being portrayed in a bad light and the mediators siding with them. If you find yourself in this situation, keep reminding the mediators that **the focus should be on the children.**

RED FLAG · is a metaphor for something signalling a problem. RED FLAGS are markers for concern. You have an ancient inbuilt warning system in your body; that GUT FEELING that tells you that you should be doing something, calling someone or perhaps you have a feeling you should go somewhere.

In other situations, you may feel that something isn't right or maybe a person is making you feel odd. This is your INTUITION. During the idealisation and DEVALUING stage, these feelings were turned off as you overlooked one RED FLAG after another.

RUMINATION · Coming out of these relationships, you have more questions than answers and easily slip into rumination. This is the process of continuously thinking about the same thoughts, which tend to be sad or dark. Rumination can be dangerous to your mental health, as it impairs your ability to think and process emotions.

SMEAR CAMPAIGN · The definition of a SMEAR CAMPAIGN is "a plan to discredit a public figure by making false accusations". Take out the phrase 'public figure' and REPLACE it with your name.

SMEAR CAMPAIGNS are designed to ensure the ABUSER looks like the VICTIM. They created stories about the terrible things you had allegedly said or done. They wanted to punish you and, as they can't take responsibility, you were the problem. This may have started before the FINAL discard. The SMEAR CAMPAIGN could have involved mutual friends, members of your family or even your children.

If you think back to the idealisation stage of your relationship, they were telling you that you were the only person who has ever fully understood them, and they were telling you stories about their exes. This was a SMEAR CAMPAIGN; they were doing the same then. You probably saw how they treated other people but believed they would never do that to you.

They might be telling similar stories about you; the awful way they were spoken to, the awful way they were treated, and they may claim you are bipolar or have an addiction.

This behaviour excites them, it gives them a sense of power and it gives them the SUPPLY they so desperately need.

SUICIDAL IDEATION · The pain of not wanting to be alive is SUICIDAL IDEATION. It is a common phenomenon in C-PTSD, particularly during intense or prolonged flashbacks. It is fantasising or thinking about wanting to die.

Perhaps you wake up in the morning realising you are still alive and wondering how you are going to get through another day. You may have thoughts where you wish you weren't alive anymore, believing there is nothing to live for. You are now left wondering how you will live without them and what there is to live for.

You might have thoughts of having an accident, stepping out in front of a car or going to sleep and never waking up again. This is passive suicidality which is not a serious intent to kill yourself.

Active suicidality is when a person is actively proceeding in the direction of taking their life. This is less common, but if you are considering actively ending your life, please seek help. The Samaritans operate a 24-hour helpline in the UK call 116 123 or in the US call 1-800-273-8255.

SUPPLY · Think of an electric car. For it to work, it needs to be plugged into an energy source, and once fully charged you can unplug it and drive off. When it starts to lose power, you plug it back in and charge it. The EMOTIONAL ABUSER needs a source of SUPPLY for them to function.

SUPPLY to the EMOTIONAL ABUSER is attention, and they surround themselves with people who can provide it to them. Their main source of SUPPLY will be from their main partner and a secondary source of SUPPLY may come from children, work colleagues and family members – or it may come from an affair.

They don't really care where it comes from, as long as the focus is on them.

THE ORIGINAL WOUND · The Original Wound is where the abuse started. It is the reason you may not have walked away when you saw the RED FLAGS and the reason others saw the abuse but you didn't. We live in a Theta state up until we are about 7 or 8 years old. This is a hypnotic state and what we see and hear during this time we take on as the truth. If the experience was not healthy, these beliefs about ourselves are carried forward. You may have been the family scapegoat or had a parent that was unavailable.

These wounds are much like a verruca, which is a virus that penetrates all the levels of the skin. If the full root isn't removed, it lays dormant until it is TRIGGERED again. And this is the same for The ORIGINAL WOUND: if you do not fully heal the wound, it will appear again, and you will keep meeting people who treat you the same way.

TRAUMA BONDING · We develop bonds for survival in childhood, usually with our caregiver, who is the foundation of attachment. When our safety is threatened in some way, we turn to them for support and protection.

TRAUMA BONDING is one of the reasons it is so hard to heal from toxic and Emotionally Abusive relationships. The damage caused puts you into a state of confusion because you had no idea the ABUSE was taking place.

When our safety is threatened in some way, we turn to our tribe for support and protection and these BONDS can be created within hours.

People who have experienced a traumatic situation together always have a BOND of survival.

BONDING is a very strong connection, and it strengthens when we spend time with someone, make love, and when we have children together.

TRAUMA BONDING is used by the Emotional Abuser or toxic person to enable them to gain power and control over you.

During the idealisation stage, they positioned themselves as the caregiver, showering you with attention, gifts, meals, days out and manufacturing a love you may never have experienced before.

They then started devaluing you, with slight put-downs and triangulation or Gaslighting. You may have rationalised their behaviour, believing they cared about you, creating even more BONDING. This was the reason you were so connected to them, and when the relationship ended, you wondered how you would survive.

TRAUMA BONDING made it hard to enforce BOUNDARIES, which was why it was so painful to stay away from them.

When they threatened your safety through their bad behaviour, you turned to them for help and protection. You rationalised their behaviour, believing they cared about you. This created further bonding, which was the reason you felt so connected to them. When the relationship finished, your stress levels were so high, you experienced FEAR and couldn't imagine your life without them.

They, on the other hand, played the VICTIM, and you very likely believed this was all your fault. The pain you now feel runs deep into your Soul.

VICTIM · Definition · *A person harmed, injured, or killed as a result of a crime, accident, or other event or action. Synonyms: sufferer, the injured party, casualty, injured person, wounded person.*

You would think that, coming out of an emotionally abusive relationship, you would be the victim – but the Abuser claims they are. They lead you to believe you were the Abuser, and during the devaluation stage, you lost your self-esteem.

When they were Triangulating you, you began to believe you weren't good enough. You saw the red flags, but they made excuses, and you were so invested in the relationship, you forgot about yourself.

During the idealisation stage, they discovered your insecurities, which they claimed were the same as theirs and later, during a discard or the final discard, they used these against you.

You are left feeling that you are to blame for the abuse, and this is completely normal. You were conditioned and groomed to absorb all of the problems in the relationship. Once you understand the role you played, you are ready to heal.

WALKING ON EGGSHELLS · This term is used to describe the way you behaved around the ABUSIVE person, being very careful not to upset them and cause a NARCISSISTIC RAGE. You tiptoed around a person or situation in order to protect yourself, your children, or those around you. You avoided saying or doing something to keep the peace, not wanting to wake up the monster.

WORD SALAD · This is a form of communication which doesn't make sense. It fails to progress the discussion in any way or creates a situation where there is no outcome. This was all done in an attempt to confuse you and gain control over the conversation and you!

These conversations didn't make sense, and when you tried to understand what was actually being said, they moved the conversation in a different direction. They brought up your wrongdoings as an attempt to cover up their behaviour, and they played the VICTIM.

MASTER TASK LIST

Use this page to save your information

Key: o event - notes • important > move to task list < cancelled

REFERENCES

1. Through The Looking Glass: Finding Light at the End of the Rabbit Hole

   https://singerburke.com/looking-glass-finding-light-end-rabbit-hole/#:~:text=The%20phrase%20
   %E2%80%9CThrough%20the%20Looking,world%20both%20recognizable%20and%20yet

2. Woman's Aid What is Coercive Control

   https://www.womensaid.org.uk/information-support/ what-is-domestic-abuse/coercive-control/

Quote References

1. https://www.goodreads.com/quotes/380221-nice-people-don-t-necessarily-fall-in-love-with-nice-people

2. https://www.goodreads.com/quotes/9657488-grief-i-ve-learned-is-really-just-love-it-s-all-the

3. Just like an egg: "Unknown

4. https://www.goodreads.com/author/quotes/14671015.Brittany_Burgunder

5. https://www.thedivorcesanctuary.com/findinglily

6. https://www.brainyquote.com/quotes/peter_a_levine_864302

7. https://drgabormate.com/the-wisdom-of-trauma/

8. https://www.goodreads.com/work/quotes/15599-the-green-mile?page=3

Image References

Photo by
Akram Huseyn on Unsplash

Photo by
Fabian Blank on Unsplash

Photo by
Hannah Olinger on Unsplash

Photo by
Humphrey Muleba on Unsplash

Photo by
visuals on Unsplash

Photo by
Eduardo Sánchez on Unsplash

Photo by
Julia Kuzenkov on Unsplash

Photo by
Jackson Simmer on Unsplash

Milton Keynes UK
Ingram Content Group UK Ltd.
UKHW050358261023
431322UK00004B/33